THE LOCH NESS MONSTER

By Emily Rose Oachs

BELLWETHER MEDIA • MINNEAPOLIS, MN

Blastoff! Discovery launches a new mission: reading to learn. Filled with facts and features, each book offers you an exciting new world to explore!

This edition first published in 2019 by Bellwether Media, Inc.

No part of this publication may be reproduced in whole or in part without written permission of the publisher. For information regarding permission, write to Bellwether Media, Inc., Attention: Permissions Department, 6012 Blue Circle Drive, Minnetonka, MN 55343.

Library of Congress Cataloging-in-Publication Data

Names: Oachs, Emily Rose, author.
Title: The Loch Ness Monster / by Emily Rose Oachs.
Description: Minneapolis, MN : Bellwether Media, Inc., 2019. |
    Series: Blastoff! Discovery: Investigating the Unexplained |
    Audience: Age 7-13. |
    Includes bibliographical references and index.
Identifiers: LCCN 2018003680 (print) | LCCN 2018006676
    (ebook) | ISBN 9781626178557 (hardcover : alk. paper)|
    ISBN 9781681035963 (ebook)
Subjects: LCSH: Loch Ness monster–Juvenile literature.
Classification: LCC QL89.2.L6 (ebook) | LCC QL89.2.L6 O225
    2019 (print) | DDC 001.944–dc23

LC record available at https://lccn.loc.gov/2018003680

Editor: Paige Polinsky   Designer: Andrea Schneider

Printed in the United States of America, North Mankato, MN.

TABLE OF CONTENTS

LOST IN THE LOCH

The water is calm as the sun rises over Scotland's **Loch** Ness. Mickey and Sam join a crew of researchers on a ship. Together, the team sets out into the water.

The researchers use **sonar** to scan the loch's deep waters. It shows a few fish swimming past. Mostly, all is quiet. But Sam and Mickey hold their cameras close. They have a feeling that this might be the day they find the Loch Ness monster.

VISITOR FROM OUTER SPACE?

Some people believe the answer to the Loch Ness monster mystery lies out of this world. They think Nessie might actually be an alien from a different planet!

In the late afternoon, the sonar picks up on something new. A large shape is moving deep underwater. It looks like it is more than 20 feet (6 meters) long! The object darts away from the boat.

sonar

105

The researchers act quickly. They turn the boat to chase the object through the loch. The sonar continues to track it for a few minutes. Then the object disappears. Mickey and Sam look at each other in shock. Did they just chase Nessie?

STRANGE SIGHTINGS AT LOCH NESS

The narrow Loch Ness cuts across 23 miles (37 kilometers) of northern Scotland's countryside. **Legends** say its deep waters hide a large, mysterious creature. Hundreds of people claim to have spotted the animal, nicknamed Nessie.

Eyewitnesses often describe seeing a snakelike body and flippers among the waves. Some spot a long neck rising from the surface. There are many **theories** about Nessie. It could be an ancient sea creature **species**. Or it could be an animal completely unknown to humans!

LOCH NESS, SCOTLAND

Loch Ness

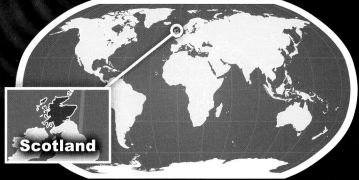

Scotland

A MYSTERY SURFACES

Loch-monster legends date far back. Ancient carvings found near Loch Ness show familiar animals like horses and birds. But a strange animal with flippers appears with them. Some believe this is Nessie! A written account from 565 CE also tells of a giant creature seen near the loch.

Major modern sightings of the Loch Ness monster began in 1933. A passing couple said they saw a huge creature in the loch. They described its whalelike body rolling in the waves. Newspapers spread the story, and interest spiked.

ancient carving

BEASTS OF SCOTTISH LEGENDS

Nessie is not the only creature said to haunt Scotland's waters. Myths tell of a ghostly water horse called a kelpie. Those who climbed onto its back would not return from the loch.

A REAL REWARD FOR A MYSTERY MONSTER

Many people wanted to capture Nessie. In 1934, New York's Bronx Zoo offered $25,000 to whoever caught the creature. Today, that reward would be worth more than $400,000!

More reported sightings trickled in. Soon, people flocked to Loch Ness with boats and cameras. They wanted to find **evidence** of the mysterious creature. One famous hunter claimed to find monster footprints. But an **investigation** soon proved the prints were fake.

the Surgeon's Photograph

In 1934, surgeon Robert Wilson drove past Loch Ness. He saw an animal's head and long neck rise from the water. Wilson snapped a grainy photo that became known as the Surgeon's Photograph. Sixty years later, it was revealed as a **hoax**. But it remains the most famous image of Nessie.

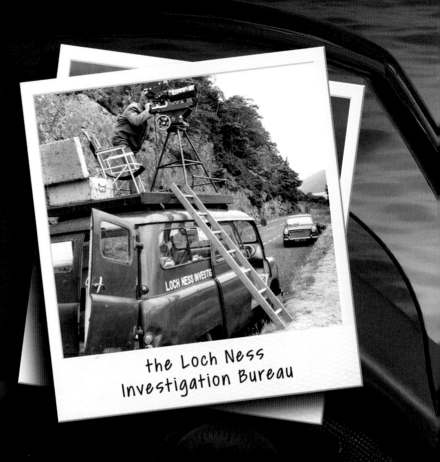

the Loch Ness
Investigation Bureau

The Loch Ness Investigation Bureau formed in the early 1960s. Members watched the loch for Nessie. Investigations dipped below the surface, too. Researchers began to use sonar technology. In 1987, Operation Deepscan brought 24 boats to Loch Ness. Their sonar mapped more than half the lake.

No investigation turned up proof of the monster's existence. But in many, sonar picked up on large moving shapes that could not be explained. Researchers often left with unanswered questions.

fish-finder sonar

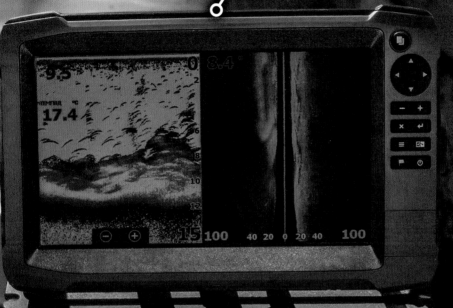

NESSIE: WANTED ALIVE

Some Nessie hunters used traps to try
to capture the sea creature alive.
One trap built in 1984 stretched
60 feet (18 meters) long!

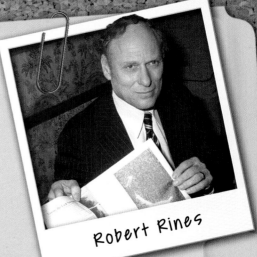

Robert Rines

PROFILE: THE FLIPPER PHOTOS

Scientist Robert Rines led a Nessie investigation in the 1970s. Rines and his team used advanced sonar. They also set up an underwater camera. Every 45 seconds, a strobe light flashed as the camera took a photo.

In 1972, Rines watched in excitement as the sonar tracked a large moving form. Three photos seemed to support the sonar's findings. They showed an unknown object. When enhanced, the object appeared to be the large flipper of a sea creature. One scientist then argued that Nessie was a prehistoric marine animal called the plesiosaur!

Plesiosaur

members of Rines'
1976 investigation

SWIMMING BESIDE
THE DINOSAURS

Plesiosaurs swam in Earth's oceans while
dinosaurs lived. The largest plesiosaur
was about 43 feet (13 meters) long. Its
neck and head made up half of this length!

SEARCHING
THE DEEP

Loch Ness is a tough place to search. In some places, the lake bottom is more than 750 feet (229 meters) below the surface. Rotting plant matter called peat makes the water extra **murky**. It can be difficult to see more than a few feet ahead.

INVESTIGATOR TOOLBOX

sonar

drone

camera

strobe light

binoculars

Researchers could **dredge** or **trawl** Loch Ness to pull evidence from its cloudy waters. But these methods might harm the loch and its occupants. Instead, Nessie hunters use tools that help them safely see into the loch's depths.

Sonars give Nessie hunters an underwater view of the loch. Fish-finders scan the area below a research boat. Side-scan devices sweep out to the sides. As the boat moves, these devices send pings of sound into the water. The pings bounce back when they strike something solid. A machine builds an image of the lake below based on the returning sounds.

Some researchers send underwater **drones** into the deepest parts of the loch. The drones use sonar to search the lake's bottom. They reach areas boats cannot.

underwater drone

HOW SONAR WORKS

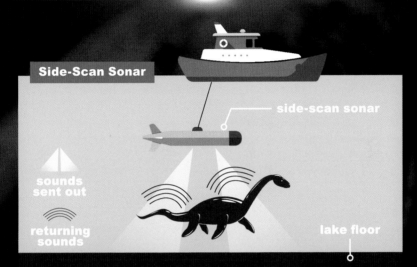

Side-Scan Sonar

side-scan sonar

sounds
sent out

returning
sounds

lake floor

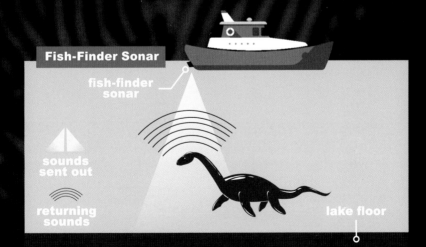

Fish-Finder Sonar

fish-finder
sonar

sounds
sent out

returning
sounds

lake floor

HUNTING FROM HOME

Cameras can share live video of Loch Ness with the world. With these webcams, a person only needs the Internet and some patience to be a Nessie hunter!

Cameras have been key equipment for Nessie hunters since the 1930s. Investigators use them to capture anything unusual that surfaces from the loch. Researchers also try to pierce the loch's dark, cloudy waters with underwater cameras and strobe lights.

underwater camera

Not all of an investigator's tools need to be high-tech. Researchers use **binoculars** to watch the waves from shore. A simple notepad and pen can help any Nessie hunter log evidence and sightings.

NESSIE NONBELIEVERS

Scientists believe people are easily tricked into seeing Nessie. A splashing **sturgeon** or floating log could be mistaken for the mysterious monster. Even sonar readings of the loch's fish or normal underwater objects could be confused for Nessie. People might be more likely to see Nessie if that is what they want to see!

floating log

sturgeon

Skeptics also point out that evidence could be faked.
In the past, some major sightings were proven to be hoaxes.
Today, computers make it easy to **edit** photos and **footage**
to fake Nessie encounters.

Some people still believe Nessie is a plesiosaur. But skeptics say plesiosaurs likely died out 65 million years ago. Loch Ness then spent thousands of years completely covered by ice. No plesiosaur could have survived.

Plesiosaur or not, eyewitness reports often describe Nessie as being at least 20 feet (6 meters) long. But there are few food sources in the loch. Skeptics argue it would be difficult for such a large sea creature to survive.

THE MYSTERY LIVES ON

Most scientists deny that the Loch Ness monster exists. Still, Nessie sightings have been on the rise. People continue to watch the waves for a glimpse of the beast.

The mystery lives on at the shores of Loch Ness. Maybe there really is a sea monster hidden away in the loch's depths. Or perhaps the loch's waters are as empty as skeptics say. For now, the question of the Loch Ness monster will remain unanswered until solid proof surfaces.

A DECADES-LONG HUNT

Steve Feltham holds the world record for longest constant search for the Loch Ness monster. Feltham set up camp beside Loch Ness in 1991. He has been watching for Nessie ever since!

GLOSSARY

binoculars—devices used to look at things that are far away

dredge—to scoop out mud and weeds from the bottom of a lake, river, or other body of water

drones—vehicles that can move around without a person inside to drive them

edit—to change, move, or remove parts of a photo or video recording

enhanced—improved or made clearer

evidence—information that helps prove or disprove something

eyewitnesses—people who see something happen firsthand

footage—video recordings

hoax—an act meant to fool or trick someone

investigation—the act of trying to find out the facts about something in order to learn if or how it happened

legends—stories from the past that are believed by many people but not proven to be true

loch—the Scottish word for lake

murky—cloudy or gloomy

prehistoric—from a time before written language existed

skeptics—people who doubt something is true

sonar—a device that uses sound waves to detect and map objects underwater

species—a group of animals or plants that are similar

strobe light—a bright light that flashes quickly

sturgeon—a type of large fish

theories—ideas based on known facts that are meant to explain something

trawl—to drag a fishing net along the bottom of a lake, river, or other body of water

TO LEARN MORE

AT THE LIBRARY

Nagle, Frances. *The Loch Ness Monster.* New York, N.Y.:
Gareth Stevens Publishing, 2017.

Peabody, Erin. *The Loch Ness Monster.* New York, N.Y.:
Little Bee Books, 2017.

Uhl, Xina M. *Loch Ness Monster.* Mankato, Minn.: Black
Rabbit Books, 2018.

ON THE WEB

Learning more about the Loch Ness
monster is as easy as 1, 2, 3.

1. Go to www.factsurfer.com.

2. Enter "Loch Ness monster" into the
   search box.

3. Click the "Surf" button and you will see a list of
   related web sites.

With factsurfer.com, finding more information is just a click away.

INDEX